Williamson W Publishing

W9-CDF-987

Kids' Easy

Quilting

Projects

TERRI THIBAULT

Illustrations by Heather Barberie

Quick Starts for Kids!™

WILLIAMSON PUBLISHING • CHARLOTTE, VERMONT

Library of Congress Cataloging-in-Publication Data

Thibault, Terri, 1954-
    Kids' easy quilting projects / Terri Thibault ; illustrations by Heather Barberie.
        p. cm. -- (Quick starts for kids!)
    ISBN 1-885593-49-X
        1. Quilting--Juvenile literature. 2. Quilting--Patterns--Juvenile literature. [1. Quilting.]
    I. Barberie, Heather. II. Title. III. Series.

    TT835 .T42 2000
    746.46--dc21

                                                                00-043495

Quick Starts for Kids!™ series editor: **Susan Williamson**
Interior design: **Linda Williamson, Dawson Design**
Interior illustrations: **Heather Barberie, Rum Raisin Designs**
Cover design: **Marie Ferrante-Doyle**
Cover illustrations: **Michael Kline**
Cover photography: **David A. Seaver**
Printing: **Capital City Press**

Williamson Publishing Co.
P.O. Box 185
Charlotte, VT 05445
(800) 234-8791

Manufactured in the United States of America

10 9 8 7 6 5 4 3

DEDICATION
To my parents, George and Jeanne, who always have nurtured my creative appetite; to my husband, Norm, for his loving support; and especially to my kindred spirit in life's adventures, my friend Peg.

CONTENTS

Quilt It Yourself!

*H*ere's a Quick Starts for Kids!™ *skill you can enjoy today and continue as a lifelong hobby! But let's clear up one thing: Quilting is* not *just about cherished old-fashioned bed coverings made by your grandmother (or your great-grandmother) when she was your age! Those are treasures, to be sure. But hey! You're a cool kid with your* own *ideas about what you like!*

And that's the great thing about quilting: You can make things as fresh as your next idea; as creative as the fabric, colors, and designs you choose; and as easy as cutting, piecing, and placing a stitch here and there! Really! You'll be totally amazed at how simple it is, how quickly you'll be making some really great projects, and how much fun you'll have. You'll be quilting in no time flat!

With quilting, you can start small and grow your projects to a size and shape you are comfortable with. And with Williamson's Quick Starts for Kids!™, you can get started in the fun of quilting from the get-go. Yes, quilting today is all about YOU and what you like!

I've been quilting with friends and with my kids for a long time now — and I can't wait to share what I know and love with you! So start at the beginning to get a few basics down, and then feel free to skip around to the projects you want to make first. And, most important, have a great time!

Kids' Top 10 Quilting Questions ... With Answers!

—1—

I've never sewn before, and I don't have a sewing machine. Can I still make these quilting projects?

You bet! No sewing machine or fancy stitches are required. All these quilting projects are specially designed for kids to make by *hand-piecing* (a fancy way for saying "sewing by hand") — just the way all those really valuable "old-fashioned" quilts were! Using patterns from this book, you trace onto the fabric, cut out the pieces, and then sew them together by hand. Each of the simple stitches is explained and illustrated so you can learn as you go. No sewing experience is needed!

—2—

What if I get stuck? (No one in my family sews much.)

Help is on the way! In fact, if you look at the how-to-do-it illustrations, you'll probably figure it out. (It's not hard at all.) If not, ask a teacher or the librarian or your next-door neighbor. Lots of people sew and quilt, so keep asking. People who are good at figuring out puzzles are usually good at putting fabric patterns together, so ask your math or graphic arts teachers, too.

—3—

I don't have much money. How much is this going to cost?

Homemade is best — and very inexpensive! Each of the projects described here requires only small amounts of fabric, batting, and thread — the rest is up to you! By making it yourself, you'll be able to pick out the fabric, colors, and designs you like best, and create a masterpiece by spending just $5 or less!

—4—

How are quilting projects different from plain old sewing?

Part of what makes a quilting project different from regular sewing is what it looks like when it's finished. Everything quilted consists of three layers: the *quilt top* (which often has a special design), the *batting* (the material that makes a quilt puffy and warm), and the *backing* (the fabric on 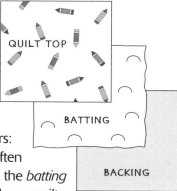the back of the quilt). All of the projects in this book have these same three layers when they are completed. The actual sewing you do involves simple stitches, but since you sew through several layers, the result is always soft and puffy!

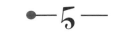

I don't know what a "seam allowance" is (Can I spend it?), and the other sewing words are all new to me, too. Does that matter?

No problem! Any stitching words (such as "seam allowance") are explained in the text or in the *Quick Starts Illustrated Stitch & How-to Dictionary*™ on pages 58–62). In no time at all, you'll be using quilting lingo like a pro! (By the way, you can't spend a seam allowance. It's just the amount of space you leave between the edge of the fabric and the stitching.)

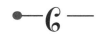

How will I know what fabric to use?

Easy-to-sew cotton prints are suggested for each project. And one of the best parts about sewing is that you get to choose the colors and the fabric design! Will yours have a glittering star motif or a sports design with printed bats and balls? Fabric stores have cotton prints in practically any color or design you could imagine.

What other supplies do I need?

Most of the pattern-making and sewing supplies are probably already around your house, but you can easily find what you need at a sewing or craft store. See the *Basic Quilting Supplies* list on page 7 for details.

Will my projects turn out nice enough to give for gifts?

The people who receive your gifts will know that they are extra-special, because you took the time to make something by hand, all by yourself — just for them! You can't ask for a more special gift than that.

What should I do with the fabric scraps?

Since many of these projects need small pieces of fabric, you'll probably be able to use the scraps from one project in a different project, or to add as decorations. Save all the extras in a "scrap bag" — they're sure to come in handy!

—10—

I have a lot of dolls and stuffed animals. Can I use any of these projects for my dolls or animals?

You sure can! The *Doll Quilt with Puppy Appliqué* (page 48) is just the right size for a doll or teddy bear bed, the *Wonderful Wall Nesters* (page 23) are perfect for displaying Beanie Babies and other treasures. And after you've tried the quilted projects here, you'll be able to come up with designs of your own. It's easy, once you get started quilting!

Quilting Basics

The most important quilting tools are *your* creativity and *your* imagination, because you're the one choosing the fabric that will make your quilted projects extra-special. So a good place to begin is to imagine what kind of fabric you want. Of course, you'll also need some matching thread and puffy batting to make the layers fluffy. *Check the materials listed at the beginning of each project to see what specific items you'll need,* so you are certain to have everything on hand before you begin.

Basic Quilting Supplies

Things you probably have at home:

- Cereal-box cardboard or heavyweight paper — for making sturdy patterns
- Chopstick, wooden spoon, or the eraser end of a pencil — for pushing out the corners of projects once you've reversed them
- Craft scissors — for cutting paper and cardboard
- Measuring tape or ruler — for drawing patterns and for measuring fabric, batting, and ribbons
- Pencil — for tracing the book patterns onto tracing paper
- Sewing needles — for hand sewing
- Straight pins — for holding fabric in place
- Tape — for piecing partial tracing-paper patterns together

Things you may need to buy:

- Batting — for adding "loft" to each project, making it cushiony
- Cotton fabric — in various prints or solids, according to each project
- Embroidery floss — for embroidering lettering or appliqué details
- Fabric glue — for gluing felt appliqués. (You can find it at any fabric or craft store under a variety of names, such as Gem-Tac or Fabri-Tac.)
- Fabric scissors (not the same as craft scissors), child-sized — for cutting fabric
- Needle threader (optional) — for extra-easy threading
- Quilting thread — a thick, sturdy thread for sewing
- Seam ripper (optional) — for easy stitch removal ('cause we all make mistakes!)
- Thimble (optional) — for pushing in the needle, sized to fit your middle finger
- Tracing or lightweight typing paper — for tracing patterns

SEWING TRICKS

• **Big needle, strong thread!** Use a needle that is easy for you to thread. The best needles for these *Quick Starts for Kids!*™ quilting projects are *crewel* needles. I recommend sizes 6–8. (The higher the number, the smaller the eye and shorter and finer the needle.) You'll also need strong *quilting thread*, so that your projects stay together for a long, long time!

• **Need help threading your needle?**
Needle threaders make it a cinch! (1) Push the wire end of the needle threader through the eye of your needle; (2) insert the thread through the wire of the threader; and (3) pull the wire back out of the needle. Now, (4) remove the threader from the thread. Your needle is threaded!

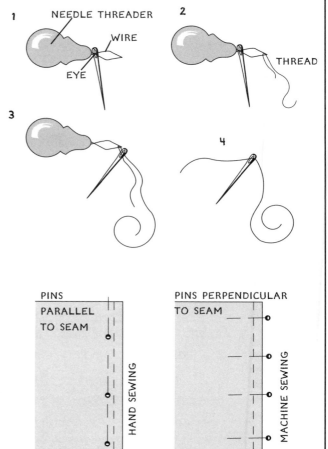

• **Pins & pinning.** Straight pins are great for holding fabric pieces together. The best straight pins for quilting (called *quilting* or *ball-point pins*) have a colored bead on top that's easy to see. When you're sewing by hand, place the pins *parallel* to the seam (in the same direction) you're sewing. If you have permission to sew by machine on some pieces, you'll want to place the pins *perpendicular* to the seam (at a right angle — horizontal to the seam).

• **Be nimble and use a thimble.** Save those fingers! Use a thimble (those little "fingertip hats") on your middle finger. Poke the needle into the fabric, give it a push with the thimble, and out it comes on the other side, easy as pie! You can get kid-sized thimbles at a sewing store.

Shopping for Fabrics

I just love choosing fabrics; in fact, I can spend hours wandering the aisles of the fabric section, checking out all the colors and patterns of the cloth.

I recommend you start with **100 percent cotton** — it's the best for a beginning quilter because it's strong and easy to work with, and it is usually fairly inexpensive, too. To find out what a fabric is made of, check the end of the *bolt*, the cardboard insert wrapped with cloth. It lists all the information you need to know about the fabric.

CHOOSING A PRINT. When you're picking out printed fabric, look for those in which the pattern can go in any direction. Stripes and other patterns with lines that need to match up when the pieces are sewn together are trickier to sew.

KNOW THE FABRIC WIDTH. Fabrics come in different widths. All of the fabric amounts that I've listed assume you're buying fabric that's 44" (110 cm) wide — the most common width. Fabric is sold by the yard (36"/90 cm), so when you buy 1/2 yard (45 cm), for example, you're getting a piece that's 18" x 44" (45 x 110 cm). Other common widths are 45" (112.5 cm) and 60" (150 cm). Wider fabrics are fine to use; your pattern layout will just look a little different and you'll have more fabric left over.

WASH FABRICS BEFORE STARTING. It's always a good idea to wash all of your fabrics once you get them home. This way, they'll shrink first, plus you can check the colors for "bleeding." (That's when some of the dye comes off, possibly staining other fabrics.) Just follow the instructions found on the fabric bolts.

All About Batting

This batting has nothing to do with baseball or softball! *Batting* is a fluffy material sold in various thicknesses, called *lofts*; you put it between your fabric layers to make your project softer and "cushiony." I've used *low-loft* batting for these projects.

Be sure to get batting, not fiberfill (loose stuffing); the packaging looks very similar. Flat sections of batting come in rolls; 36" x 45" (90 x 112.5 cm) or 45" by 60" (112.5 x 150 cm) are common sizes.

Butterfly Pincushion

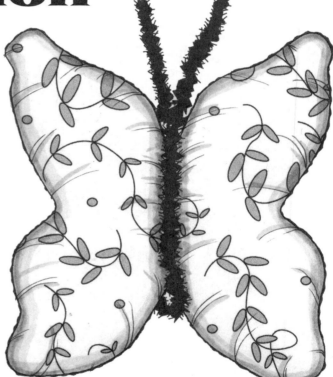

Butterflies mean
summer — my favorite
season! This easy-to-make
quilted version makes a great
pincushion — a very
handy item for quilters
or anyone who sews.

Materials to make a *Quick Starts*™ Butterfly Pincushion:

- *Pattern-making supplies:* pencil, ruler or straightedge, tracing paper, cardboard, craft scissors
- *Sewing supplies:* pencil or chalk, straight pins, fabric scissors, needle and matching thread
- Cotton print fabric: $1/4$ yard (9"/22.5 cm)
- Batting: 7" x 7" (17.5 x 17.5 cm)
- Pipe cleaner

   NOTE: The finished pincushion measures about $4^1/2$"x $4^1/2$" (11.5 x 11.5 cm). All SEAM ALLOWANCES are $1/2$" (1 cm).

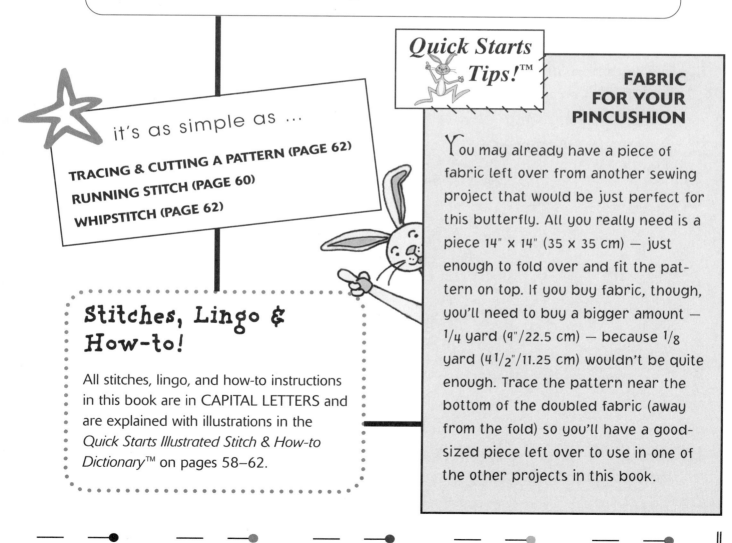

it's as simple as …

TRACING & CUTTING A PATTERN (PAGE 62)

RUNNING STITCH (PAGE 60)

WHIPSTITCH (PAGE 62)

Stitches, Lingo & How-to!

All stitches, lingo, and how-to instructions in this book are in CAPITAL LETTERS and are explained with illustrations in the *Quick Starts Illustrated Stitch & How-to Dictionary*™ on pages 58–62.

Quick Starts Tips!™

FABRIC FOR YOUR PINCUSHION

You may already have a piece of fabric left over from another sewing project that would be just perfect for this butterfly. All you really need is a piece 14" x 14" (35 x 35 cm) — just enough to fold over and fit the pattern on top. If you buy fabric, though, you'll need to buy a bigger amount — $1/4$ yard (9"/22.5 cm) — because $1/8$ yard ($4^1/2$"/11.25 cm) wouldn't be quite enough. Trace the pattern near the bottom of the doubled fabric (away from the fold) so you'll have a good-sized piece left over to use in one of the other projects in this book.

Making the Pattern

1. Using a pencil, trace the BUTTERFLY pattern (page 15) onto tracing paper, including the 1 1/2" (4 cm) center line, and cut it out.

2. Trace the tracing-paper butterfly shape onto the cardboard and cut out that pattern, making a stiffer butterfly pattern (which is easier to work with when you're cutting fabric). Transfer the center line. Label it "BUTTERFLY" and mark the number of pieces you'll need to cut — two fabric and one batting.

Cutting the Fabric and Batting

1. Fold the fabric in half, RIGHT SIDES TOGETHER. Center it on the batting.

DOUBLE THICKNESS OF FABRIC

SINGLE THICKNESS OF BATTING

2. Place the cardboard BUTTERFLY on top of the fabric. (Don't worry, you're not making an inside-out butterfly! When you reverse it later, the print will be on the outside and the batting on the inside, just the way you want it.)

3. Holding the pattern firmly in place, trace around it on the fabric. Remove the pattern. Pin the three layers together to hold them in place.

4. Cut along the traced line through all three layers. Mark the center line on the top piece of fabric.

Kids' Easy Quilting Projects

FABRIC: RIGHT OR WRONG?

Every piece of fabric has two sides: a WRONG and a RIGHT. No, the fabric hasn't done anything good or bad. The *right* side looks like the finished material, such as the bright, printed side of a cotton print. The *wrong* side is the faded side of the fabric or the backing, like the inside-out side of a shirt or dress.

When making projects in this book, the cutting and sewing are usually done with the RIGHT SIDES TOGETHER, which means they face against each other when your fabric is folded. It's easier to see traced patterns on the lighter, wrong side, and then when you turn the stitched seams to the inside (so they won't show), the right sides face out — just the way you want them to! See the *Quick Starts Illustrated Stitch & How-to Dictionary*™ (page 58–62) for clear definitions of the terms.

SEWING THE BUTTERFLY

Sew around the edge (stitching through all three layers) with a RUNNING STITCH.

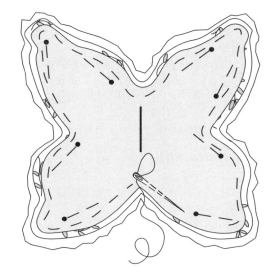

Quick Starts Jump Starts!™

What's the hardest thing about quilting? Getting your fabric and batting stacked so that when you turn it inside out, the fabric is RIGHT SIDES OUT and the batting is in the middle.

The trick is to visualize, or picture in your mind, how you want the project to look when you are done. And then keep in mind that you'll be turning it inside out *after* you sew it. So the stitching and rough edges won't show and the batting will be hidden in the middle!

DON'T FORGET!
Knot the end of your thread when sewing!

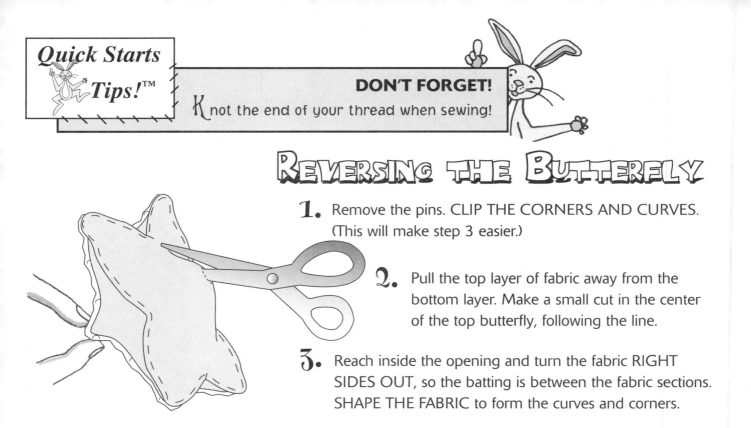

REVERSING THE BUTTERFLY

1. Remove the pins. CLIP THE CORNERS AND CURVES. (This will make step 3 easier.)

2. Pull the top layer of fabric away from the bottom layer. Make a small cut in the center of the top butterfly, following the line.

3. Reach inside the opening and turn the fabric RIGHT SIDES OUT, so the batting is between the fabric sections. SHAPE THE FABRIC to form the curves and corners.

STITCHING THE OPENING

1. Fold the open edges into the butterfly, RIGHT SIDES TOGETHER. Pin the opening closed.

2. WHIPSTITCH the opening shut.

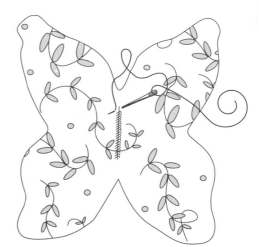

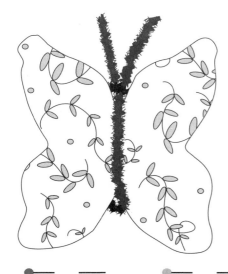

Finishing Touches

Adding Antennae
Fold the pipe cleaner in half. Place it around the center of the butterfly and twist together to define the body and form antennae.

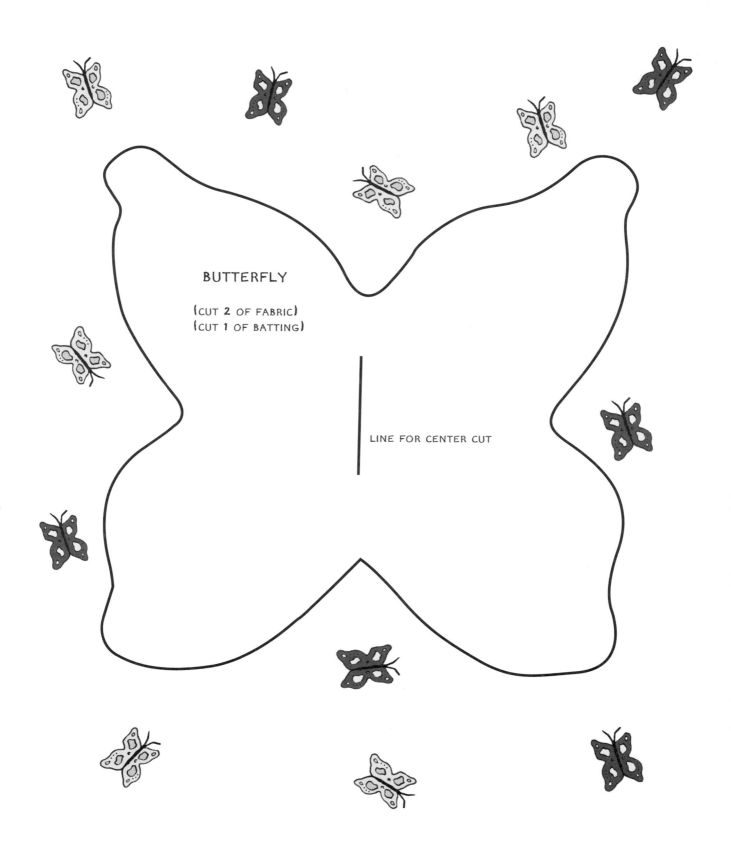

BUTTERFLY

(CUT **2** OF FABRIC)
(CUT **1** OF BATTING)

LINE FOR CENTER CUT

Tic-Tac-Toe on the Go!

FRONT

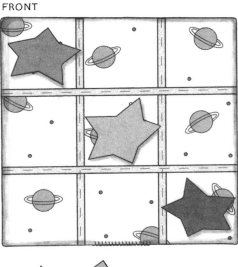

BACK

POCKET

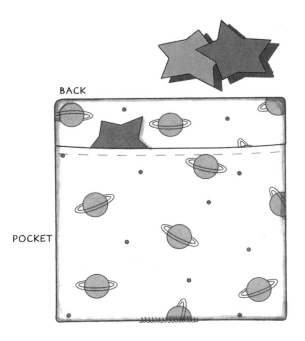

PLAYING
PIECE

This quilted Tic-Tac-Toe "board" is easy to make, easy to carry, and fun to play at home, too! The batting makes it stiff enough for a good game board and the secret pocket on the back stores the playing pieces. Just ask me — my kids and I play this game in the car all the time!

Materials to make Tic-Tac-Toe on the Go:

✗ *Pattern-making supplies:* pencil, ruler or straightedge, tracing paper, tape, cardboard, craft scissors

✗ *Sewing supplies:* pencil or chalk, straight pins, fabric scissors, needle and matching thread, ruler or measuring tape

✗ Cotton print fabric: $1/3$ yard (12"/30 cm)

✗ Batting: 12" x 12" (30 x 30 cm)

✗ Ribbon: 1 yard (1 m) of $1/4$" (5 mm) width

✗ Self-sticking Velcro dots

✗ 2 colors of Foamtastic craft foam or other material (for playing pieces)

✗ Tacky glue

NOTE: The finished game board is 8" x 8" (20 x 20 cm).
All SEAM ALLOWANCES are $1/2$" (1 cm).

it's as simple as ...

TRACING & CUTTING A PATTERN (PAGE 62)
RUNNING STITCH (PAGE 60)
WHIPSTITCH (PAGE 62)

Making the Patterns

Trace the POCKET pattern (page 22) twice onto tracing paper. Cut out the pieces and tape them together to make a full-sized pattern. Repeat for the BOARD pattern (page 22). Trace the completed patterns onto cardboard; cut them out and label them.

1. Fold the fabric in half, RIGHT SIDES TOGETHER. Place it on the batting, lining up the bottom edges. Place the BOARD pattern on the fabric close to the bottom edge as shown, and trace the outline.

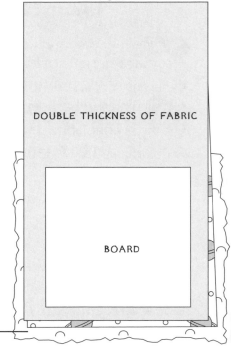

FOLD

DOUBLE THICKNESS OF FABRIC

BOARD

2. Pin all three layers together to hold them in place. Cut along the traced line through all the layers so you end up with two fabric BOARD pieces and a matching batting piece.

SINGLE THICKNESS OF BATTING

3. Open the remaining fabric piece and place it RIGHT SIDE DOWN. Trace the POCKET pattern onto the WRONG SIDE of the fabric. Cut along the traced line.

SINGLE THICKNESS OF FABRIC

RIGHT SIDE DOWN

POCKET

EDGING THE POCKET

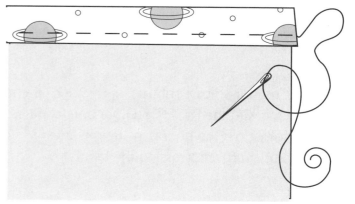

1. Fold the top side of the POCKET fabric piece down about 1/2" (1 cm), as shown.

2. Pin or FINGER-PRESS the folded edge in place and stitch, using a RUNNING STITCH. Set aside.

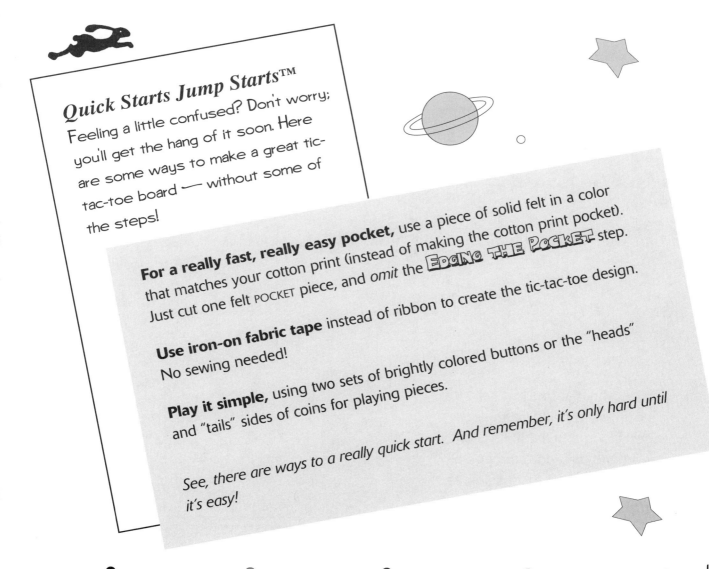

Quick Starts Jump Starts™

Feeling a little confused? Don't worry; you'll get the hang of it soon. Here are some ways to make a great tic-tac-toe board — without some of the steps!

For a really fast, really easy pocket, use a piece of solid felt in a color that matches your cotton print (instead of making the cotton print pocket). Just cut one felt POCKET piece, and *omit* the EDGING THE POCKET step.

Use iron-on fabric tape instead of ribbon to create the tic-tac-toe design. No sewing needed!

Play it simple, using two sets of brightly colored buttons or the "heads" and "tails" sides of coins for playing pieces.

See, there are ways to a really quick start. And remember, it's only hard until it's easy!

Putting on the Tic-Tac-Toe Design

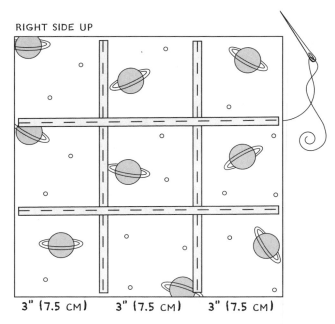

RIGHT SIDE UP

3" (7.5 CM) 3" (7.5 CM) 3" (7.5 CM)

1. Cut four strips of ribbon, each 9" (22.5 cm) long. On the RIGHT SIDE of one fabric BOARD, pin the ribbon in straight lines, 3" (7.5 cm) apart, crisscrossing the fabric.

2. Using a RUNNING STITCH, sew along the middle of each ribbon piece.

Making the Fabric "Sandwich"

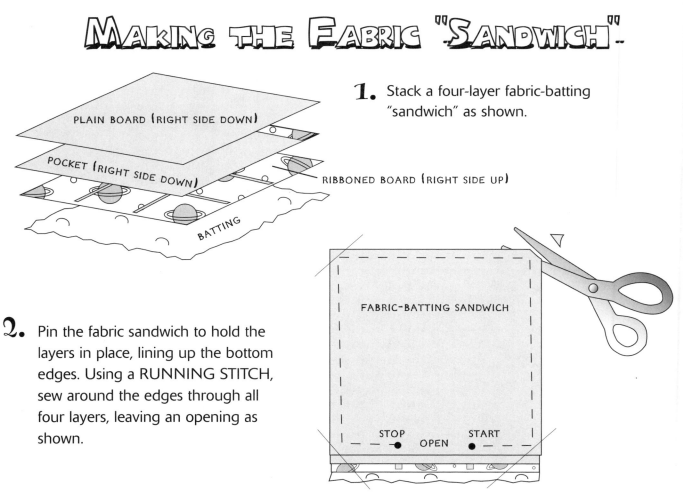

PLAIN BOARD (RIGHT SIDE DOWN)

POCKET (RIGHT SIDE DOWN)

RIBBONED BOARD (RIGHT SIDE UP)

BATTING

1. Stack a four-layer fabric-batting "sandwich" as shown.

2. Pin the fabric sandwich to hold the layers in place, lining up the bottom edges. Using a RUNNING STITCH, sew around the edges through all four layers, leaving an opening as shown.

FABRIC-BATTING SANDWICH

STOP   OPEN   START

3. CLIP THE CORNERS and turn the fabric sandwich RIGHT SIDES OUT, so the batting is *between* the fabric sections. SHAPE THE FABRIC.

4. Fold the fabric edges along the opening to the inside and pin. WHIPSTITCH the opening closed.

A BATTING & FABRIC SANDWICH

It's sometimes tricky to figure out how to sandwich the batting and fabric so that the completed project has the batting on the *inside* and the RIGHT SIDE of the fabric on the *outside*. Follow the diagram carefully, and remember to *visualize* how it will look when you turn it inside out!

Finishing Touches ◎

VELCRO SELF-STICKING DOTS

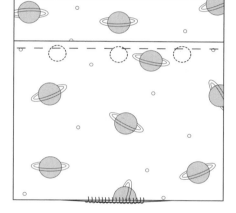

BACK

Adding the Velcro Closures

1. Stick the Velcro dots (fuzzy and looped sides) together.

2. Place the stick-on sides inside at the top of the pocket so that one side is against the board fabric and the other side is against the inside of the pocket.

3. Make Tic-Tac-Toe playing pieces and put them in the pocket.

Create Your Own Playing Pieces!

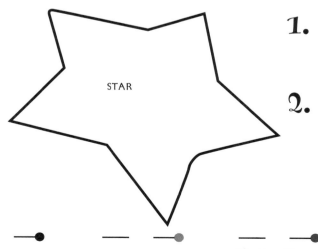

STAR

1. Make the cardboard STAR pattern. Trace it onto two colors of Foamtastic craft foam, making nine of each color.

2. Cut out the shapes and glue one of each color together, so that you have nine playing pieces with a different color on each side. After the glue dries completely, play away! The winner is the first one to get three in a row!

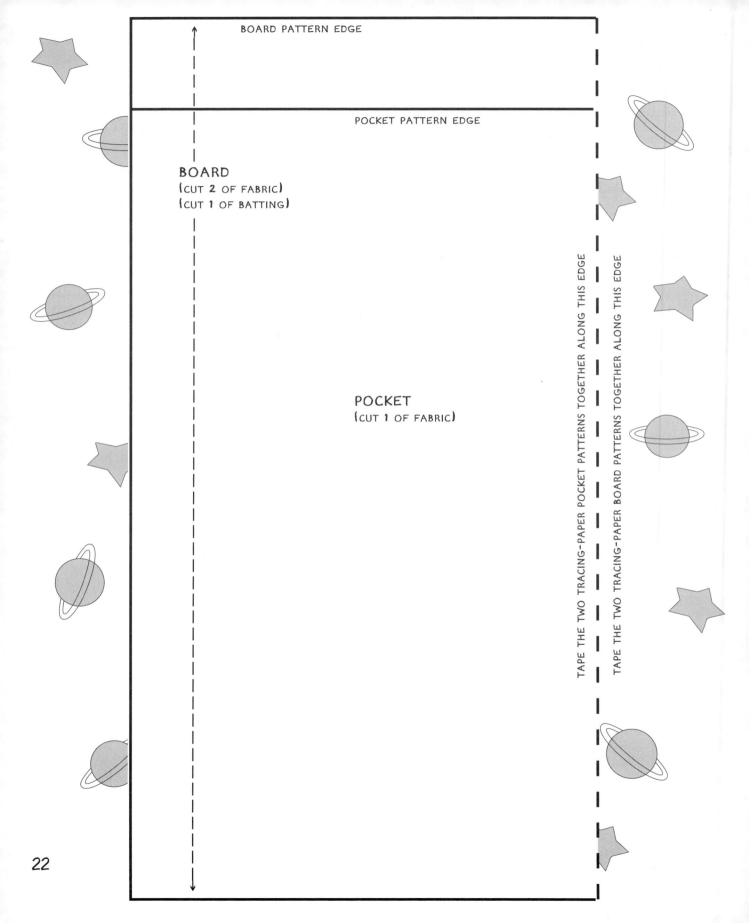

BOARD PATTERN EDGE

POCKET PATTERN EDGE

BOARD
(CUT **2** OF FABRIC)
(CUT **1** OF BATTING)

POCKET
(CUT **1** OF FABRIC)

TAPE THE TWO TRACING-PAPER POCKET PATTERNS TOGETHER ALONG THIS EDGE

TAPE THE TWO TRACING-PAPER BOARD PATTERNS TOGETHER ALONG THIS EDGE

Wonderful Wall Nesters

In my home, we each have collections: animals, Matchbox cars, marbles, toys, buttons, coins, trading cards, and all sorts of stuffed animals. To make sure we don't lose any of our treasures, we store them in specially made Wall Nesters. You can hang the nesters together on the wall for easy access, or take them down and button them shut to make a handy travel pouch!

Materials to make one Wall Nester:

- *Pattern-making supplies:* pencil, ruler or straightedge, tracing paper, cardboard, craft scissors
- *Sewing supplies:* pencil or chalk, straight pins, fabric scissors, needle and matching thread, ruler or measuring tape
- Cotton print fabric: 1/4 yard (9"/22.5 cm)
- Batting: 12" x 20" (30 x 50 cm)
- Ribbon: 7" (17.5 cm) of 1/4" (5 mm) width
- Button

NOTE: The finished Wall Nester is 5$\frac{1}{2}$" x 5$\frac{1}{2}$" (14 x 14 cm) when closed. All SEAM ALLOWANCES are 1$\frac{1}{2}$" (1 cm).

it's as simple as ···

TRACING & CUTTING A PATTERN (PAGE 62)
RUNNING STITCH (PAGE 60)
WHIPSTITCH (PAGE 62)

MAKING THE PATTERNS

Trace and then cut out the WALL NESTER and POCKET patterns (page 28). Now, trace, cut out, and label the two cardboard patterns.

CUTTING THE FABRIC & BATTING

1. Fold the fabric in half, RIGHT SIDES TOGETHER. Place it on the batting, lining up the bottom edges. Place the WALL NESTER and POCKET patterns on the fabric as shown and trace the outlines.

2. Pin all three layers together to hold them in place. Cut along the traced lines through all the layers. Now you have two fabric pieces and one batting piece for each pattern.

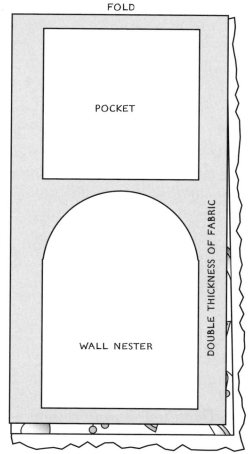

FOLD

POCKET

WALL NESTER

DOUBLE THICKNESS OF FABRIC

SINGLE THICKNESS OF BATTING

Quick Starts Jump Starts™
If you want to make a lot of Wall Nesters, here's a way to start quickly — and a quicker finish! (And it's a lot easier, too.)

For a really fast, really easy pocket, use a piece of solid felt in a color that matches your cotton print (instead of making the quilted pocket). Just cut one felt POCKET piece. Then sandwich it between the two Wall Nester fabric pieces, as shown on page 27 in "This 'Sandwich' Is a Double-Decker!" You won't need to cut any pocket batting or make a pocket sandwich, and you'll have fewer layers to stitch through in the final steps. Go for it!

ATTACHING THE RIBBON

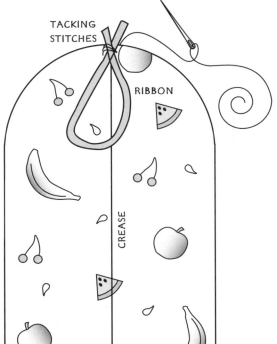

1. Fold one of the WALL NESTER fabric pieces in half lengthwise. FINGER-PRESS down the fold to make a crease; then, open the fabric, RIGHT SIDE UP.

2. Fold the ribbon in half, making a 3" (7.5 cm) loop and place the *ends* of the ribbon at the top of the crease (they'll hang over the edge of the fabric a bit). Using a TACKING STITCH, sew three stitches through the ribbon ends and the WALL NESTER fabric piece to hold the ribbon in place.

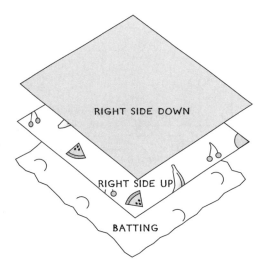

MAKING THE POCKET "SANDWICH"

1. Stack a three-layer fabric-batting "sandwich" as shown.

2. Pin the layers to hold; then, sew the top edge with a RUNNING STITCH.

3. Remove any pins and turn the fabric sandwich RIGHT SIDES OUT, so the batting is *between* the two POCKET fabric sections.

1. Now, make a second fabric sandwich as shown, stacking the POCKET sandwich and remaining pieces as shown.

2. Pin the layers together lining up the bottom edges. Using a RUNNING STITCH, sew all of the layers together, starting in one corner and stitching around the curve to the other corner, leaving the bottom open.

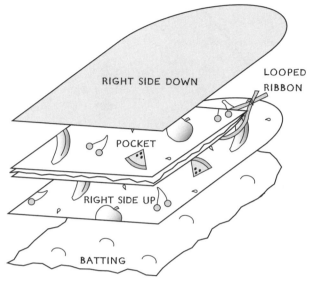

RIGHT SIDE DOWN

LOOPED RIBBON

POCKET

RIGHT SIDE UP

BATTING

OPENING AT BOTTOM

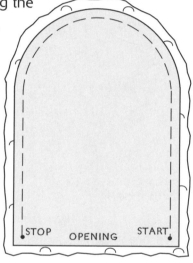

STOP   OPENING   START

3. CLIP THE CURVES and remove the pins. Turn the fabric RIGHT SIDES OUT, so that the batting is *between* the fabric sections and the POCKET is on the *outside*. SHAPE THE FABRIC.

4. Fold the fabric edges along the opening to the inside and pin. WHIPSTITCH the opening closed.

5. Sew a button (page 61) onto the bottom of the POCKET front.

Finishing Touches

Add Pizzazz!
Use decorative buttons that complement the fabric design in your Wall Nester. You can even buy buttons in fancy shapes, such as moons, stars, or hearts!

Making a Smaller Loop
Tie a knot in the loop to shorten it slightly and make the opening smaller to better fit the button.

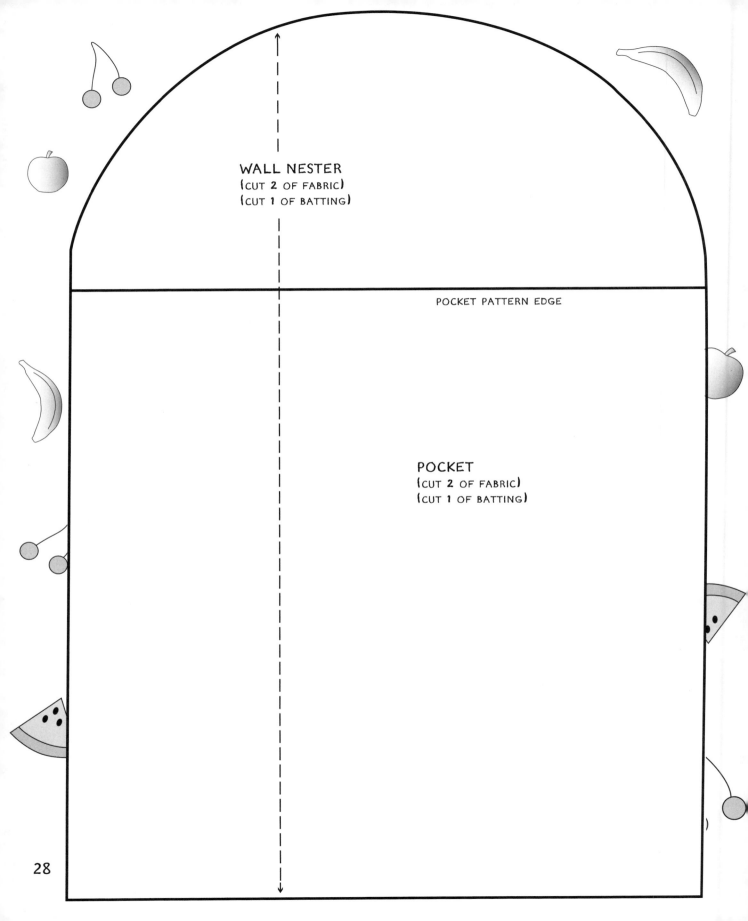

WALL NESTER
(CUT **2** OF FABRIC)
(CUT **1** OF BATTING)

POCKET PATTERN EDGE

POCKET
(CUT **2** OF FABRIC)
(CUT **1** OF BATTING)

28

Moon & Stars Mobile

Do you like gazing at the twinkling stars — and looking for the Big Dipper and the Little Dipper in the night sky? Well, with this great mobile, you can watch the stars, even when it's cloudy!

Materials to make a
Moon & Stars Mobile:

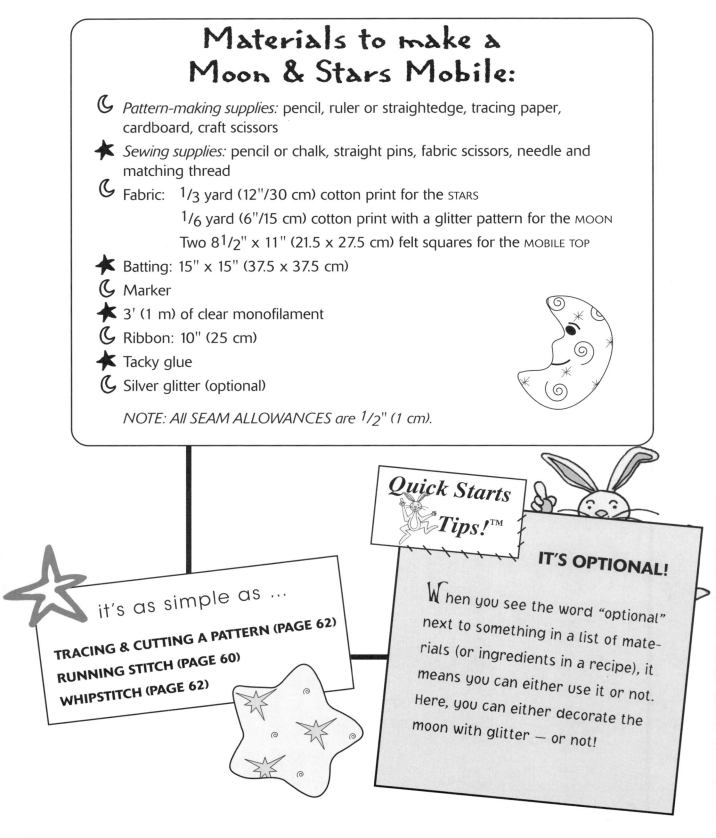

☾ *Pattern-making supplies:* pencil, ruler or straightedge, tracing paper, cardboard, craft scissors

★ *Sewing supplies:* pencil or chalk, straight pins, fabric scissors, needle and matching thread

☾ Fabric: 1/3 yard (12"/30 cm) cotton print for the STARS

1/6 yard (6"/15 cm) cotton print with a glitter pattern for the MOON

Two 8 1/2" x 11" (21.5 x 27.5 cm) felt squares for the MOBILE TOP

★ Batting: 15" x 15" (37.5 x 37.5 cm)

☾ Marker

★ 3' (1 m) of clear monofilament

☾ Ribbon: 10" (25 cm)

★ Tacky glue

☾ Silver glitter (optional)

NOTE: All SEAM ALLOWANCES are 1/2" (1 cm).

it's as simple as ...
TRACING & CUTTING A PATTERN (PAGE 62)
RUNNING STITCH (PAGE 60)
WHIPSTITCH (PAGE 62)

Quick Starts Tips!™

IT'S OPTIONAL!

When you see the word "optional" next to something in a list of materials (or ingredients in a recipe), it means you can either use it or not. Here, you can either decorate the moon with glitter — or not!

Kids' Easy Quilting Projects

Making the Patterns

Trace and then cut out the STAR, MOON, and MOBILE TOP patterns (pages 34–36). Now, trace, cut out, and label the three cardboard patterns. Mark the dots on the STAR and MOON patterns.

Cutting the Fabric & Batting

THE FABRIC:

1. Fold the moon fabric and the star fabric in half, both with RIGHT SIDES TOGETHER. Trace the MOON pattern on the moon fabric. Trace the STAR pattern three times on the star fabric.

2. Pin the moon fabric layers together and the star fabric layers together to hold them in place. Cut along the traced lines through *both* layers of each fabric, so that you have two MOON pieces and six STAR pieces. Mark the dots on the WRONG SIDE of each fabric piece.

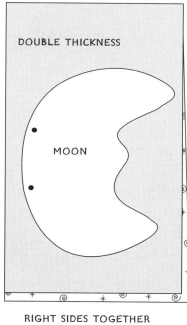

FOLD

DOUBLE THICKNESS

MOON

RIGHT SIDES TOGETHER

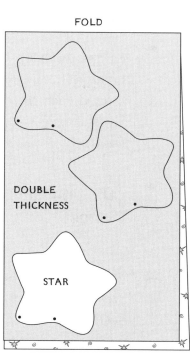

FOLD

DOUBLE THICKNESS

STAR

RIGHT SIDES TOGETHER

THE BATTING:

1. With the marker, trace the MOON pattern once and the STAR pattern three times on the single layer of batting.

2. Cut out the batting shapes.

Moon & Stars Mobile

Making the Moon & Stars "Sandwiches"...

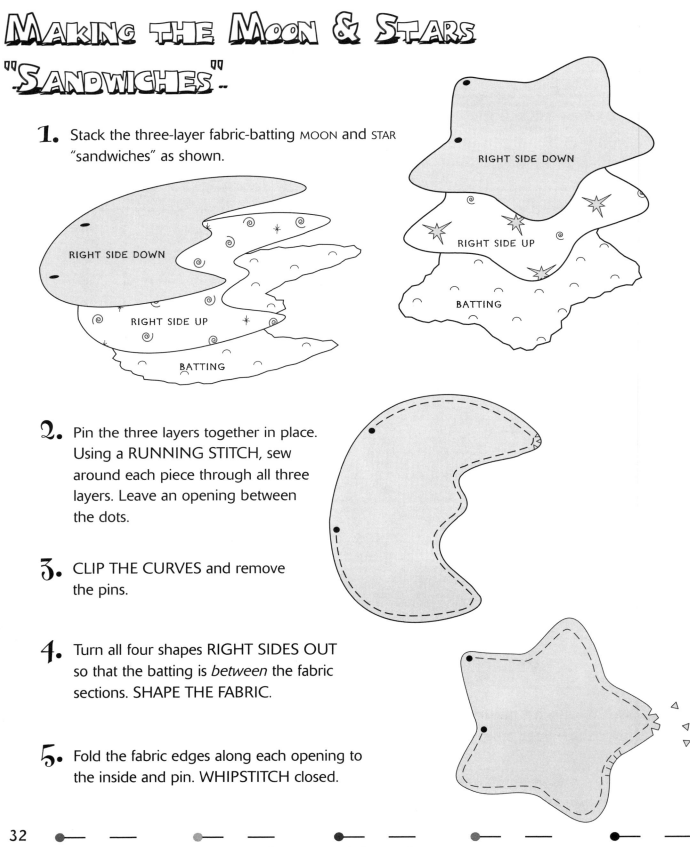

1. Stack the three-layer fabric-batting MOON and STAR "sandwiches" as shown.

   RIGHT SIDE DOWN

   RIGHT SIDE DOWN

   RIGHT SIDE UP

   RIGHT SIDE UP

   BATTING

   BATTING

2. Pin the three layers together in place. Using a RUNNING STITCH, sew around each piece through all three layers. Leave an opening between the dots.

3. CLIP THE CURVES and remove the pins.

4. Turn all four shapes RIGHT SIDES OUT so that the batting is *between* the fabric sections. SHAPE THE FABRIC.

5. Fold the fabric edges along each opening to the inside and pin. WHIPSTITCH closed.

Making the Mobile

1. Stack the felt squares. Trace the MOBILE TOP pattern onto the top felt piece. Cut out the felt shapes and glue one felt piece to each side of the cardboard pattern.

2. To attach a ribbon hanger, fold the ribbon in half and tie the two ends together in a knot. Using a TACKING STITCH, sew the ribbon to the middle of the MOBILE TOP.

3. Cut the monofilament into four pieces. Knot one end and using the TACKING STITCH, sew it to one point of a finished STAR. Attach the other end of the thread to one of the points of the MOBILE TOP by inserting the needle through the felt and knotting that end.

4. Attach the two remaining STARS and the MOON to the other corners of the MOBILE TOP, adjusting the heights of the hanging shapes to balance the mobile as you go.

Quick Starts Tips!™

TYING THE MONOFILAMENT

Monofilament is more slippery than regular cotton thread, so it comes untied more easily. Try using a DOUBLE KNOT to secure it.

BALANCING YOUR MOBILE

Hold it by the ribbon hanger, and adjust the lengths of monofilament for the stars and the moon *before* you knot the lines. Just move the monofilament on the stars or moon up or down until the top of the mobile looks flat.

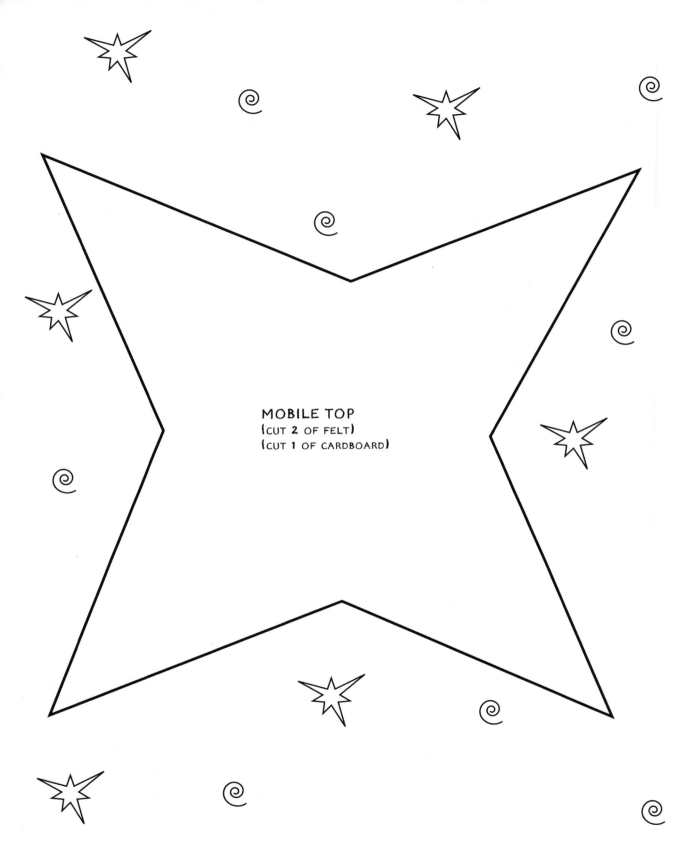

MOBILE TOP
(CUT 2 OF FELT)
(CUT 1 OF CARDBOARD)

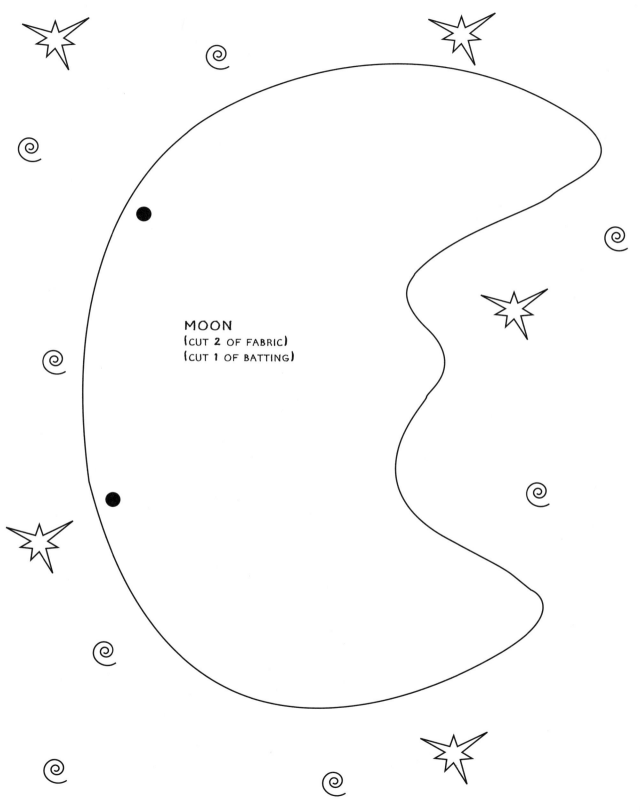

MOON
(CUT **2** OF FABRIC)
(CUT **1** OF BATTING)

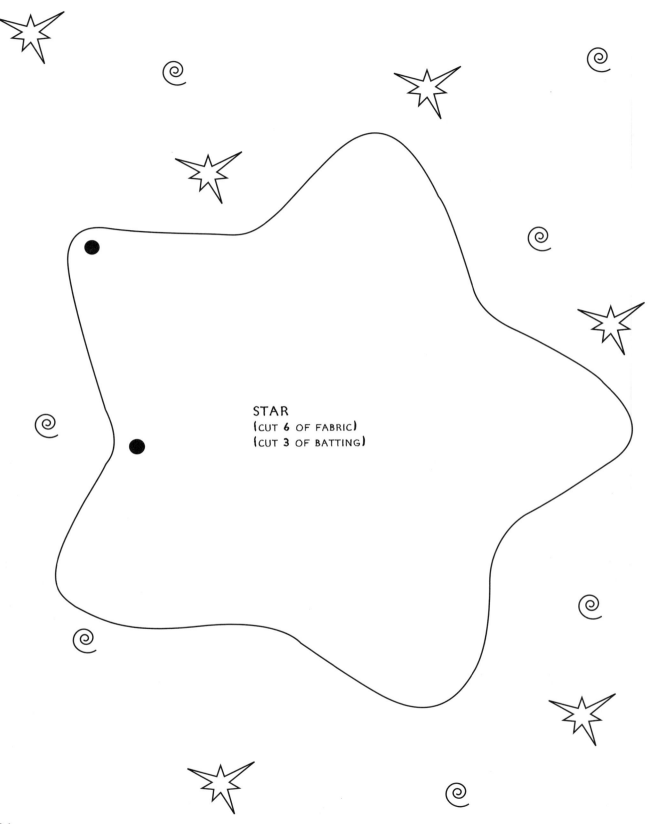

STAR
(CUT **6** OF FABRIC)
(CUT **3** OF BATTING)

Friendship Pillow

Here's an original way to show you care to a friend who's sick (or maybe injured in a soccer game): Make a personalized pillow! Piece together panels of fabric in your friend's favorite colors, and then have the whole gang sign their names with fabric markers on the front (and add silly messages on the back). This makes a great present for slumber parties, too!

Materials to make a Friendship Pillow:

- *Pattern-making supplies:* pencil, ruler or straightedge, tracing paper, tape, cardboard, craft scissors
- *Sewing supplies:* pencil or chalk, fabric scissors, straight pins, needle and matching thread
- Fabric: 1 yard (36"/90 cm) white or solid-colored cotton for PILLOW A, PILLOW B, and PILLOW BACK

  1/3 yard (12"/30 cm) cotton print for PILLOW C and PILLOW D
- Batting: 10" x 15" (25 x 37.5 cm)
- Quilter's disappearing marking pen
- Fabric pens or fabric paint, for signatures
- Pillow form or insert: 16" x 16" (40 x 40 cm), available at craft stores

NOTE: The finished Friendship Pillow is 17" x 17" (42.5 x 42.5 cm).
All SEAM ALLOWANCES are 1/2" (1 cm).

it's as simple as …

TRACING & CUTTING A PATTERN (PAGE 62)
BASTING STITCH (PAGE 58)
RUNNING STITCH (PAGE 60)
WHIPSTITCH (PAGE 62)

Quick Starts Jump Starts™

Don't know which fabrics to choose? Sometimes there are so many choices in the store that it's overwhelming!

I recommend using white or a very light color for your PILLOW A and PILLOW B sections so the signatures will show up clearly. If you use a color, look for a print that has that same color in the pattern.

Making the Patterns

1. Trace the PILLOW A pattern (page 46) four times onto tracing paper. Cut out the pieces and tape them together to make a full-sized pattern. Trace the PILLOW D (page 47) pattern three times and tape together as indicated. Trace the PILLOW B pattern (page 47) once. (You won't need a pattern for the PILLOW BACK.)

2. Trace the completed patterns onto cardboard; cut them out and label them.

Cutting the Fabric & Batting

PILLOWS A AND B:

1. Fold the white fabric in half, RIGHT SIDES TO-GETHER. Trace the PILLOW A and PILLOW B patterns as shown to be sure you'll have enough fabric left for the PILLOW BACK (you will need *two* tracings of PILLOW B).

2. Pin the layers together. Cut out the three fabric sections — you'll have a total of six fabric pieces.

3. Unpin the remaining solid fabric and unfold it, leaving the RIGHT SIDE DOWN. Set it aside for the PILLOW BACK.

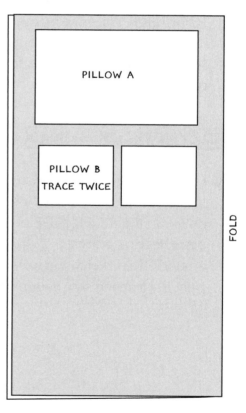

PILLOW A

PILLOW B
TRACE TWICE

FOLD

Quick Starts Tips!™

CONFUSED?

You only need one pattern piece to cut out both the B and C sections. You'll use it to cut out four pieces of the solid fabric (PILLOW B) and two pieces of the print fabric (PILLOW C).

Friendship Pillow

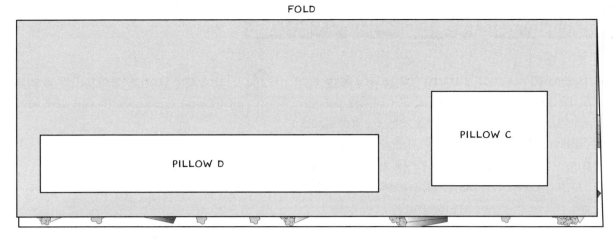

FOLD

PILLOW C

PILLOW D

PILLOWS C AND D:

Fold the print fabric in half, RIGHT SIDES TOGETHER. Place the PILLOW C and the PILLOW D patterns on the fabric and trace around them. Pin the layers together and cut out the pieces.

THE BATTING:

Place the PILLOW A pattern on the batting and trace around it; then cut.

DESIGNING THE LETTERING

1. Use the disappearing marking pen and a ruler to draw a line about two thirds of the way down on the RIGHT SIDE of one PILLOW A piece, leaving at least a 2" (5 cm) margin all around. Then sketch the words My Friends. Here is a lettering style you might try.

My Friends

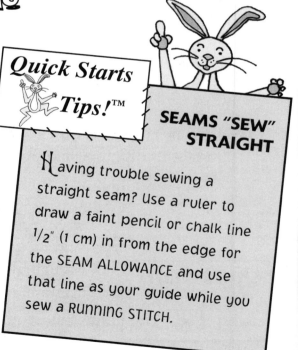

Quick Starts Tips!™

SEAMS "SEW" STRAIGHT

Having trouble sewing a straight seam? Use a ruler to draw a faint pencil or chalk line ¹/₂" (1 cm) in from the edge for the SEAM ALLOWANCE and use that line as your guide while you sew a RUNNING STITCH.

2. When you're pleased with the lettering, write over it with fabric pens or fabric paint. Let dry completely (overnight is best).

NOW YOU SEE IT ...

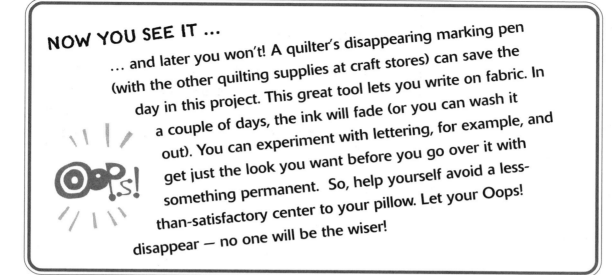

... and later you won't! A quilter's disappearing marking pen (with the other quilting supplies at craft stores) can save the day in this project. This great tool lets you write on fabric. In a couple of days, the ink will fade (or you can wash it out). You can experiment with lettering, for example, and get just the look you want before you go over it with something permanent. So, help yourself avoid a less-than-satisfactory center to your pillow. Let your Oops! disappear — no one will be the wiser!

Making the Pillow Front

SEWING PILLOW A:

Stack a three-layer fabric-batting "sandwich" as shown. Pin the layers together and then using the BASTING STITCH, sew all the way around the edges. Remove the pins. Set this piece aside until later.

PILLOW A FABRIC WITH LETTERING (RIGHT SIDE UP)

BATTING

PILLOW A FABRIC (RIGHT SIDE DOWN)

BASTING STITCH

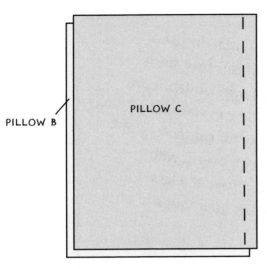

PILLOW B

PILLOW C

SEWING PILLOW B & C:

1. Place one piece of PILLOW C (print fabric) on top of one piece of PILLOW B (solid fabric), RIGHT SIDES TOGETHER. Pin the right-hand edges together and sew with a RUNNING STITCH. Remove the pins.

2. Open the pieces. FINGER-PRESS the seam so it lies flat.

3. Place a second PILLOW B piece on top of the sewn PILLOW C, RIGHT SIDES TOGETHER. Pin the unsewn edges. Sew with a RUNNING STITCH. Remove the pins.

PILLOW B

PILLOW B

PILLOW C

Quick Starts Tips!™

CONFUSED?

Look back at the illustration of the finished pillow (page 37), and you'll see at a glance how the front pieces all fit together!

4. Open the pieces and FINGER-PRESS the seam so it lies flat. Your B-C-B panel should look like this:

PILLOW B

PILLOW C

PILLOW B

5. Repeat steps 1 through 4 with the remaining PILLOW B and PILLOW C fabric pieces to form a second panel.

SEWING THE SECTIONS TOGETHER:

1. Place one B-C-B panel on top of the PILLOW A section, RIGHT SIDES TOGETHER. Pin together along the top edge. Sew with a RUNNING STITCH. Remove the pins.

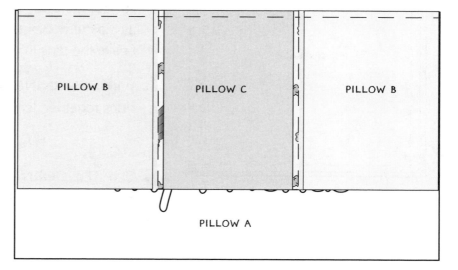

PILLOW B   PILLOW C   PILLOW B

PILLOW A

2. Open the pieces and FINGER-PRESS the seam so it lies flat.

3. Repeat steps 1 and 2 to sew the other B-C-B panel to the *bottom* of PILLOW A.

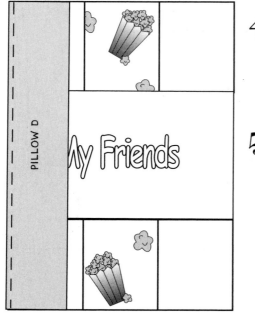

PILLOW D

My Friends

4. Place one PILLOW D piece on top of the center section, RIGHT SIDES TOGETHER. Pin together along the left-hand edge. Sew with a RUNNING STITCH. Remove the pins.

5. Repeat step 4 to sew the other PILLOW D onto the right-hand edge.

Way to go! The front of your pillow is now all sewn together! Now you'll use it as your pattern to cut out the PILLOW BACK.

Friendship Pillow

Sewing the Front to the Back

PILLOW BACK

LEAVE THIS SIDE OPEN

1. Center the PILLOW FRONT on the PILLOW BACK fabric, RIGHT SIDES TOGETHER. Pin the layers together and cut out the back, using the edges of the PILLOW FRONT as a pattern. Be careful not to cut the PILLOW FRONT! Leave the pins in place.

2. With a RUNNING STITCH, sew three sides together, leaving one side open.

3. CLIP THE CORNERS and turn your pillowcase RIGHT SIDES OUT. SHAPE THE FABRIC.

4. Slip the pillow form into the pillowcase. Fold the fabric edges along the opening to the inside, pinning them together as you go. Sew the edge closed with a WHIPSTITCH.

My Friends

Kids' Easy Quilting Projects

stretch your creative muscles!

Embroider the signature section.
Instead of coloring the letters with a fabric marker, you can embroider their outlines with an easy embroidery stitch called the BACKSTITCH (page 58) before you sew the pillow front together.

Cut a piece of embroidery thread about 24" (61 cm) long. See how it's made up of six strands? You'll need to separate them into two sections of three strands each before you thread your needle.

You can use the same color thread for all the letters, or change colors with each letter. It's your choice!

Friendship Pillow

PILLOW A
(CUT **2** OF FABRIC)
(CUT **1** OF BATTING)

TRACE FOUR TIMES AND TAPE TOGETHER
LIKE THIS:

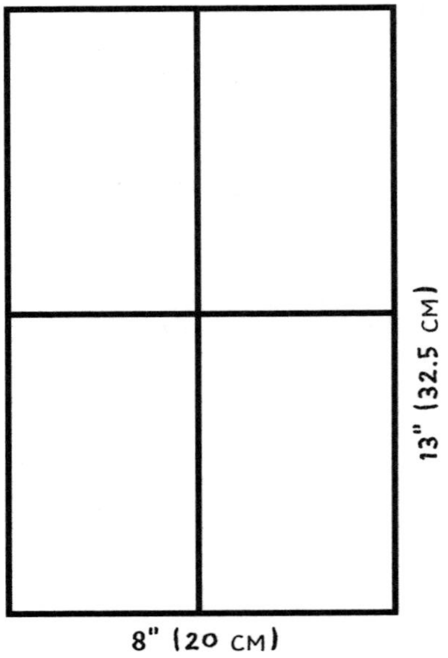

8" (20 CM)

13" (32.5 CM)

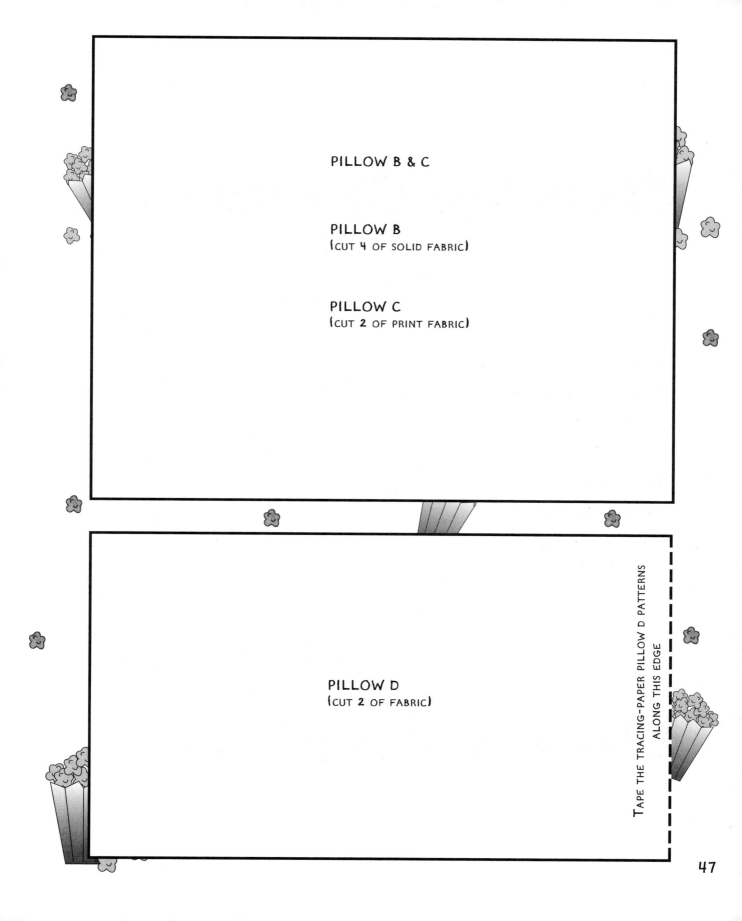

PILLOW B & C

PILLOW B
(CUT 4 OF SOLID FABRIC)

PILLOW C
(CUT 2 OF PRINT FABRIC)

PILLOW D
(CUT 2 OF FABRIC)

TAPE THE TRACING-PAPER PILLOW D PATTERNS ALONG THIS EDGE

Doll Quilt with

The puppy on this quilt has a twinkle in his eye, and he'll keep your favorite doll warm and cozy in her bed on those chilly nights! Or you can hang it on the wall.

Puppy Appliqué

Materials to make a Doll Quilt with Puppy Appliqué:

Pattern-making supplies: pencil, ruler or straightedge, tracing paper, tape, cardboard, craft scissors

Sewing supplies: pencil, white chalk, fabric scissors, straight pins, needle and matching thread, fabric glue

Fabric: 1 1/4 yards (45"/112.5 cm) cotton print fabric for the BORDER A, BORDER B, and the QUILT BACK

1/3 yard (12"/30 cm) solid-color cotton fabric for the CENTER PANEL

14" x 16" (35 x 40 cm) precut section of brown felt for the PUPPY BODY and TAIL

5" x 5" (13 x 13 cm) piece of black felt for the EARS and NOSE

Small piece of red felt for the TONGUE

Batting: 18" x 22" (45 x 55 cm)

Black fabric marker

NOTE: The finished Doll Quilt is 14" x 18" (35 x 45 cm). All SEAM ALLOWANCES are 1/2" (1 cm).

it's as simple as ...

TRACING & CUTTING A PATTERN (PAGE 62)

BASTING STITCH (PAGE 60)

WHIPSTITCH (PAGE 62)

MAKING THE PATTERNS

1. Trace the BORDER 1 pattern (page 55) twice onto tracing paper. Cut out the pieces and tape them together to make a full-sized pattern. Repeat for the BORDER 2 pattern (page 55). Trace the CENTER PANEL pattern (page 56) four times. Cut out and tape the pieces together as noted. Trace the PUPPY BODY, EAR, NOSE, TONGUE, and TAIL patterns (page 57). Cut them out.

2. Trace the completed patterns onto cardboard; cut them out and label them. Mark the two dots on BORDER 1.

CUTTING THE FABRIC

BORDERS 1 AND 2:

1. Fold the print fabric for the BORDERS in half, RIGHT SIDES TOGETHER. Place the BORDER 1 and BORDER 2 patterns on the fabric as shown and trace around them.

2. Pin the fabric layers together to hold them in place. Cut out the fabric borders and mark the two dots on the WRONG SIDE of one BORDER 1 piece. Set aside the remaining print fabric to use for your QUILT BACK.

THE CENTER PANEL:

Lay the solid fabric for the CENTER PANEL RIGHT SIDE DOWN. Trace the PANEL pattern onto the fabric; cut it out.

THE PUPPY:

1. Trace the PUPPY BODY and TAIL patterns onto the brown felt. Cut out both pieces.

2. Trace the EAR and NOSE patterns onto the black felt using white chalk. Then, trace the EAR pattern again. Cut out all three pieces.

3. Trace the pattern for the TONGUE on the red felt and cut it out.

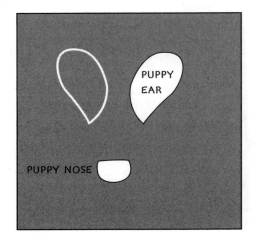

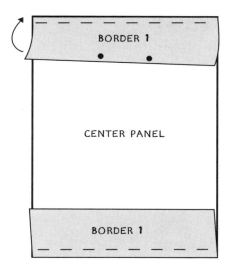

SEWING THE QUILT FRONT

1. Place one BORDER 1 fabric (the piece with two dots marked) along the top of the CENTER PANEL, RIGHT SIDES TOGETHER. Pin the edges together; sew with a RUNNING STITCH. Remove the pins.

2. Repeat step 1 to sew the second BORDER 1 piece onto the bottom edge of the CENTER PANEL.

3. Open up the pieces and FINGER-PRESS the seams so they lie flat.

4. Place one BORDER 2 piece along one side of the opened CENTER PANEL, RIGHT SIDES TOGETHER. Pin the edges together and sew with a RUNNING STITCH. Remove the pins.

5. Repeat step 4 to sew the second piece of BORDER 2 onto the other edge of the CENTER PANEL. Open up the pieces and FINGER-PRESS the seams so they lie flat.

Quick Starts Tips!™

CONFUSED?

Just look back at the illustration of the finished quilt (page 48), and you'll see at a glance how the borders attach to the center panel.

Great! Your QUILT FRONT is all sewn together!

Now you'll use it as your pattern to cut out the batting and the QUILT BACK!

Making the Fabric "Sandwich"

1. Place the sewn QUILT FRONT and the remaining QUILT BACK fabric, RIGHT SIDES TOGETHER, on the batting as shown. Pin together and cut out the back, using the edges of the QUILT FRONT as a pattern. Be careful not to cut the QUILT FRONT! Leave the pins in place.

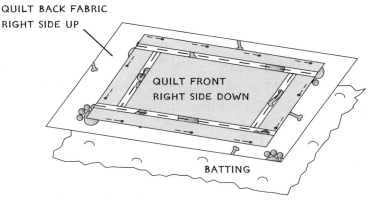

QUILT BACK FABRIC RIGHT SIDE UP

QUILT FRONT RIGHT SIDE DOWN

BATTING

2. Using a RUNNING STITCH, sew around the quilt through all three layers, leaving a small opening between the dots.

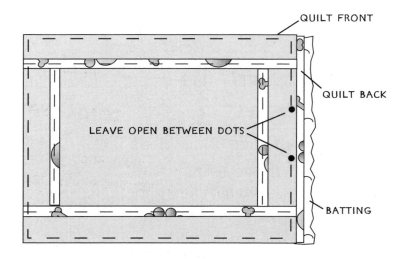

QUILT FRONT

QUILT BACK

LEAVE OPEN BETWEEN DOTS

BATTING

Kids' Easy Quilting Projects

3. Remove the pins and CLIP THE CORNERS. Turn the quilt RIGHT SIDES OUT. SHAPE THE FABRIC.

4. Fold the fabric edges along the opening to the inside and pin. WHIPSTITCH closed.

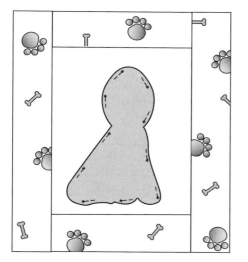

1. Pin the PUPPY BODY into the middle of the CENTER PANEL. Lightly trace the outline. Remove the pins and glue the BODY in place.

2. Glue the TAIL in place.

3. Pencil in the eyes and mouth on the puppy face. Pin the EARS, NOSE, and TONGUE in place and trace around them lightly with chalk. Remove the pins and glue each piece in place.

4. Use the fabric marker to draw the legs, mouth, and eyes.

Doll Quilt with Puppy Appliqué

your creative muscles!

• **Want to APPLIQUÉ the puppy** just like a real quilting pro? Pin the body in place and then WHIPSTITCH around the edges, kind of like sewing on a big patch, instead of gluing them. Now, WHIPSTITCH on the ears.

• **The BACKSTITCH** is an easy embroidery stitch that you can use to outline the puppy's body once it's appliquéd or glued on to give it a beautifully finished look! You can use black embroidery thread or choose a bright color for contrast.

EMBROIDERY BASICS

You can use the same-sized needle for embroidery that you've been using to sew — just thread it with *embroidery floss*, a multistrand cotton thread that comes in a rainbow of colors.

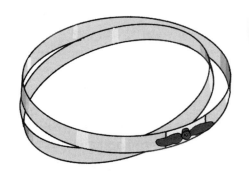

Another handy item is an *embroidery hoop* — either the wood or plastic kind. It keeps your fabric flat and your stitches even. Based on the thickness of your fabric, you may have to adjust your hoop by turning a screw on the outer ring. You also can use a self-adjusting spring-loaded hoop made of metal.

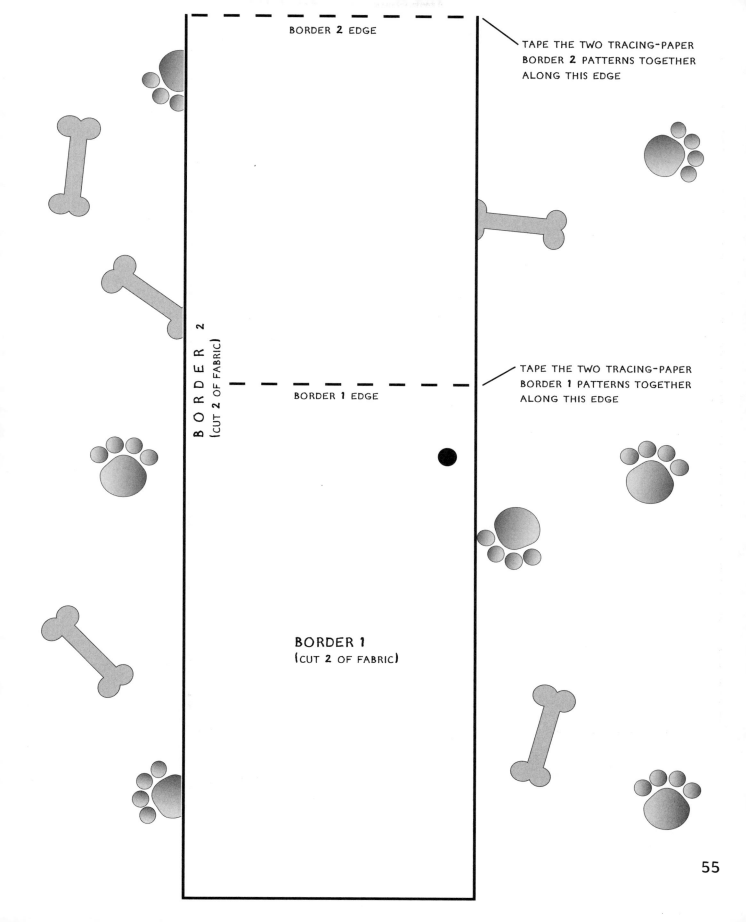

BORDER **2** EDGE

TAPE THE TWO TRACING-PAPER BORDER **2** PATTERNS TOGETHER ALONG THIS EDGE

BORDER **2** (CUT **2** OF FABRIC)

BORDER **1** EDGE

TAPE THE TWO TRACING-PAPER BORDER **1** PATTERNS TOGETHER ALONG THIS EDGE

BORDER **1** (CUT **2** OF FABRIC)

CENTER PANEL
(CUT 1 OF FABRIC)

11" (27.5 CM)

15" (37.5 CM)

TRACE FOUR TIMES
AND TAPE TOGETHER
LIKE THIS:

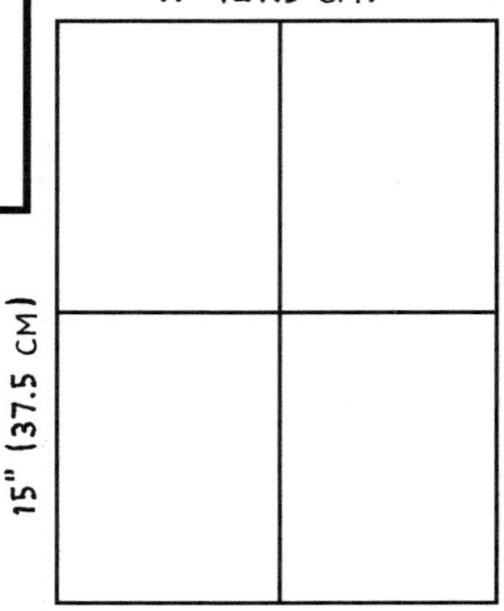

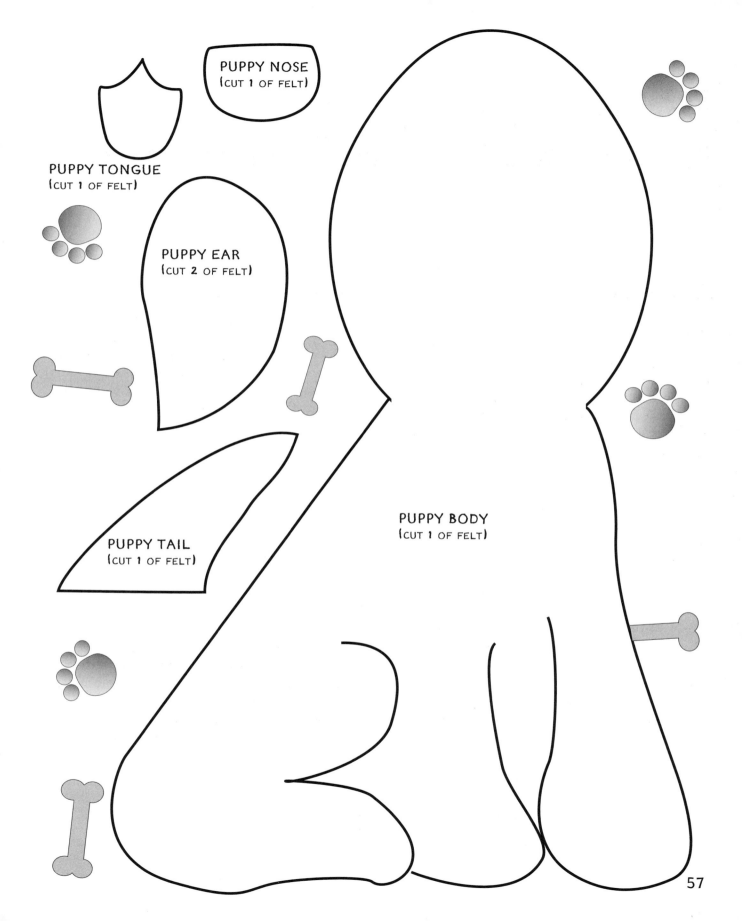

PUPPY NOSE
(CUT 1 OF FELT)

PUPPY TONGUE
(CUT 1 OF FELT)

PUPPY EAR
(CUT 2 OF FELT)

PUPPY BODY
(CUT 1 OF FELT)

PUPPY TAIL
(CUT 1 OF FELT)

57

Illustrated Stitch & How-to Dictionary™

Appliqué

To *appliqué* is a fancy way of saying that you're going to decorate your finished project by sewing fabric shapes onto it. In this book, I use a simplified version of appliqué with felt shapes that you just glue on, like the puppy on the Doll Quilt (page 48). Or you can WHIPSTITCH your shapes in place.

Backstitch

This stitch is handy when you want to embroider words on a piece of fabric, such as for the Friendship Pillowcase (page 37), or outline an APPLIQUÉ like the puppy on the Doll Quilt (page 48).

To start: Knot the thread and bring the needle up through the fabric. Now, take a small backward stitch *behind* the thread. Bring the needle up *ahead* of the thread, and pull the thread through. Continue in the same pattern, always starting each stitch *behind* the previous one, until the whole edge is outlined.

To anchor the stitches when you're done: Sew over the last stitch again.

Basting Stitch

This is a temporary stitch that you use to sew two pieces of fabric together quickly to be sure they fit properly before you do your final stitching. The basting stitch is very similar to the RUNNING STITCH but the stitches are longer (at least $1/4$" to $1/2$"/.5 to 1 cm).

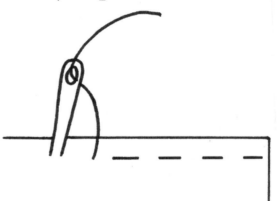

To start: Thread your needle with a long piece of thread but don't knot it. Bring your needle up through both pieces of fabric and make big, quick stitches. Leave about 6" (15 cm) of unknotted thread hanging on each end so you can easily pull the basting stitches out after your final stitching.

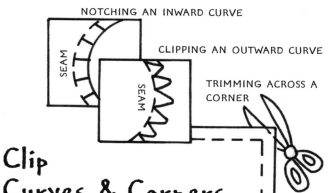

NOTCHING AN INWARD CURVE

SEAM

CLIPPING AN OUTWARD CURVE

SEAM

TRIMMING ACROSS A CORNER

Clip Curves & Corners

Cutting some of the extra batting and fabric away from the curves and corners once they're stitched is a handy way to make them lie smoothly when you turn the finished piece RIGHT SIDES OUT. Be careful not to clip too close to the seam, though!

- For seams that curve *outward:* Make little snips in the seam allowance.
- For seams that curve *inward:* Make little notches.
- For *corners:* Trim across.

Double Knot

Use this sturdy knot to secure monofilament and to knot the two ends of the thread when you DOUBLE-THREAD THE NEEDLE.

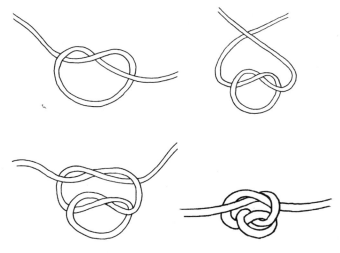

Double-Thread the Needle

This just means you thread your needle and knot the two ends together to form a double strand of thread for extra strength.

Finger-Press

You don't need an iron to flatten your fabric most of the time. All you need to do is press your finger down on the side of the seam or down the fold of the fabric to make a temporary crease.

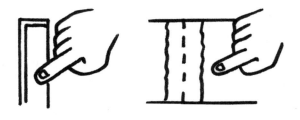

Right Side & Right Side UP

The side of a fabric where the color or pattern is brighter is the RIGHT SIDE. When the directions say to place the fabric RIGHT SIDE UP, this brighter side should be facing you. This is also the side that should be showing when you're finished.

Right Side DOWN

The brighter side of the fabric should be facing your work surface, and the WRONG SIDE (the lighter side) of the fabric should be facing you.

Right Sides OUT

After you sew a quilted shape or section together, you'll turn it so that the right sides of the fabric pieces face out toward you.

Right Sides TOGETHER

The two fabrics are placed so that the brighter sides are touching.

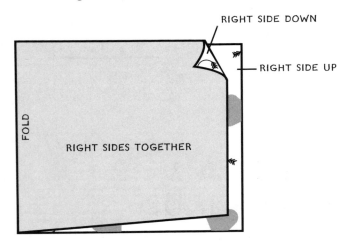

RIGHT SIDE DOWN

RIGHT SIDE UP

FOLD

RIGHT SIDES TOGETHER

Running Stitch

Just as its name suggests, this stitch gives you a chance to make several stitches in a hurry! It's similar to the BASTING STITCH, but uses shorter, more even stitches because it's permanent. You feed the needle in and out to make several stitches at a time (think of the needle and thread "running" through the fabric), instead of pulling the thread all the way through with each stitch.

To start: Knot the thread and bring the needle through the fabric. Now, work the tip of the needle in and out of the fabric to create three or four stitches and then pull the thread through all the stitches. Continue in this way until you finish the seam.

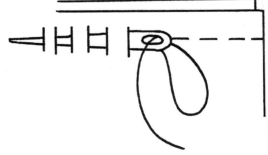

Seams & Seam Allowances

The SEAM is the stitched line that is formed by your thread when you sew two pieces of fabric together. The SEAM ALLOWANCE is the space between the seam and the edges of the fabric. In each of these projects, I've made the seam allowance $1/2$" (1 cm). That means that when you're sewing your pieces together, sew $1/2$" (1 cm) in from the edges of the fabric.

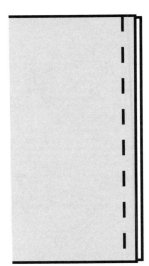

Sewing on a Button

To start: Thread the needle and knot the two ends together for a double strand. Bring the needle up from the underside of the fabric to where you want to sew on the button and run the thread through one of the holes in the button. Pull the thread all the way through. Insert the needle through another hole in the button and down through the fabric again. Repeat this up-and-down motion, sewing through all the button holes at least three times.

To finish: Wrap the thread three times around the threads between the button and the fabric. Insert the needle close to the threads and pull it through to the underside of the fabric. Knot the thread and cut it.

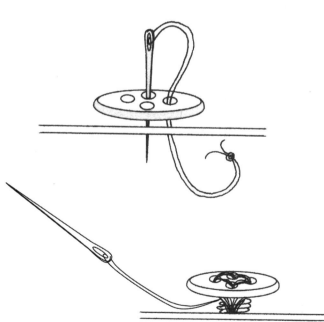

Shape the Fabric

After you've turned your project RIGHT SIDES OUT, you'll need to shape the seams, especially on the curves and corners. Use the handle of a wooden spoon, a chopstick, or the eraser end of a pencil to *gently* push along the insides of the seams so all the edges are smooth and evenly filled with batting.

Tacking Stitch

This is a very simple stitch made three or four times to attach something to a piece of fabric, like the loop of ribbon on the Moon & Stars Mobile (page 29). A few tacking stitches are also handy to reinforce the fabric wherever it might be strained — where the ribbon is tied to make a loop for the Wonderful Wall Nesters (page 23), for example.

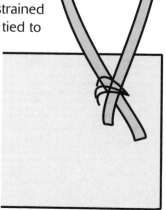

Tracing & Cutting a Pattern

To make and use the patterns in this book, you'll first need to trace them.

1. Use a pencil to trace the shape from the book onto tracing paper. Use craft scissors to cut out the traced shape.

2. Place the tracing-paper pattern onto cardboard and trace around it.

3. Cut out the cardboard pattern and label it. Mark any dots or lines shown in the book onto your cardboard pattern.

4. Store your cardboard patterns in a labeled envelope or zip-locking plastic bag. That way, you can use them many times!

Whipstitch

The WHIPSTITCH is used to close up an opening once you have turned your project RIGHT SIDES OUT, such as when sewing together the turned-under edges of the finished Tic-Tac-Toe on the Go (page 21) board.

To start: Bring the needle from the WRONG SIDE of the fabric to the RIGHT SIDE to hide the knot. Now, insert the needle through both pieces of fabric, pulling the thread all the way through so that it pulls the two edges together. Continue stitching with small tight stitches along the opening until the seam is sewn.

You can also use the whipstitch to APPLIQUÉ a design on fabric, like the puppy on the Doll Quilt (page 48).

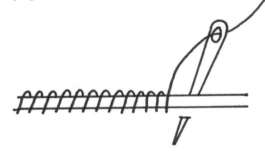

To hide the knot in the last stitch when you're appliquéing: Insert the needle to the inside, just under the top layer of fabric, making a loop. Run the threaded needle through the loop, and pull the end tightly. Carefully cut the thread close to the fabric. The end of the thread should disappear under the top fabric.

Wrong Side

See RIGHT SIDE & RIGHT SIDE OUT (page 59).

Index

More Good Books from
WILLIAMSON PUBLISHING

Please see below for ordering information or to visit our website. Thank you.

The following *Quick Starts for Kids!*™ books for ages 8 to adult are each 64 pages, fully illustrated, trade paper, 8 x 10, $7.95 US.

DRAW YOUR OWN CARTOONS!
by Don Mayne

KIDS' EASY KNITTING PROJECTS
by Peg Blanchette

KIDS' EASY QUILTING PROJECTS
by Terri Thibault

MAKE YOUR OWN TEDDY BEARS & BEAR CLOTHES
by Sue Mahren

Parents' Choice Approved
KIDS' ART WORKS!
Creating with Color, Design, Texture & More
by Sandi Henry, $12.95

American Bookseller Pick of the Lists
Dr. Toy Best Vacation Product
KIDS' CRAZY ART CONCOCTIONS
50 Mysterious Mixtures for Art & Craft Fun
by Jill Frankel Hauser, $12.95

Parents' Choice Approved
Parent's Guide Children's Media Award
MAKING COOL CRAFTS & AWESOME ART!
A Kids' Treasure Trove of Fabulous Fun
by Roberta Gould, $12.95

To see what's new at
Williamson,
learn about our *Little Hands*®,
Kids Can!®, *Kaleidoscope Kids*®,
Good Times™, and
Tales Alive!® books,
and learn more about
specific books,

VISIT OUR WEBSITE
at
www.williamsonbooks.com